Integrating My Shadow

Shadow Work Prompt Companion Journal

This book is dedicated to you!
You are a beautiful person on a journey of self acceptance and I want you to know that I see you and I accept you!

The companion shadow workbook:
Embracing My Shadow
With full exercises, meditation and inner child connection activities is available on Amazon

For more content from the creator of this journal head to https://linktr.ee/uncensoredintuition

Shadow work is a journey to accept and integrate all the aspects of ourselves that we see as unlovable, unworthy, dark or shameful. Things like greed, being "too much" and personality traits that might be unacceptable in society's twisted rule book. By doing shadow work you are allowing those hidden aspects of yourself to be visible and accepted by the only person who matters, YOU!

The "shadows" are things that you hide, not only from others, but also yourself. Often the shadows are formed in childhood or by trauma which causes us to develop a coping skill that becomes undesirable in adulthood. These unhealthy coping skills cause us to feel shame, guilt, anxiety, etc. They cause us to develop limiting beliefs and subconscious programs. These limiting beliefs, traits and subconscious programming can get in the way of many things. Biases and prejudices we may have that we don't even realize until we begin this journey. When practicing Law of Attraction, limiting beliefs prevent manifestations from manifesting. When practicing magic or intention setting those subconscious programs can block your intention.

Not a fan of people with money because they are selfish or spend frivolously? That's a trigger, journal into where that programming came from.

Do you get upset when someone chooses to disregard your advice? Another trigger, journal about why you care what other people do.

Avoiding chores? Trigger. More journaling!

With the help of this journal and the *Embracing My Shadow Workbook*, you will begin noticing patterns in your behavior that make you ask yourself *Why do I do that?*

When I set goals (that I need to convince myself I actually want to achieve) inside I really feel...

If a dark part of me were to speak it's truth right now, this is what it would say:

_____

_____

_____

_____

_____

_____

_____

_____

_____

_____

_____

_____

_____

_____

_____

_____

_____

What is my favorite thing about my life right now? What fear is associated with it and why?

Something negative that I can't stop saying to myself is…
Why am I holding on to this thought?

_____

_____

_____

_____

_____

_____

_____

_____

_____

_____

_____

_____

_____

_____

_____

_____

What does healthy competition look like? What does toxic competition look like? How does that make me feel?

When my feelings are dismissed I feel like _____.
These are some examples_____.

_____

_____

_____

_____

_____

_____

_____

_____

_____

_____

_____

_____

_____

_____

_____

These are some of the negative traits I have learned from my father:

These are some of the negative traits I have learned from my mother:

How can I give others a level of comfortability, space, and acceptance to be themselves around me?

When I think of the term "superiority complex" I think of _____ because...

If I could say one thing to the person who's hurt me most right now, I would say
_____ because _____.

What do I currently envy in someone else's life, why?

Why is it sometimes difficult to tell the difference between someone saying something intentionally mean and someone just saying something accidentally thoughtless?

Write a thoughtful letter, filled with understanding, compassion, and love to yourself when you were at your most toxic state.

When I think of the word 'punishment' I think of _____ because:

What is the one thing I know I need to do but keep avoiding? Why? How will I feel if I finish it?

This is something terrible I have wanted to tell someone to make them feel hurt.
This is how I feel about it now:

I feel isolated when _____ this is what I do about it_____.

This is the most important thing I have lost recently:

When I see people express aggressive emotions like anger or rage this is how it feels to me:

This is a list of my insecurities, I will sit with these until tomorrow:

This is a list of the things I am most secure about:

When comparing my insecurities to the things I'm secure about, I see they are different in these ways:

This is a time when I was extremely discouraged by someone else's words and how I felt:

In what areas of my life do I expect other people to conform to my beliefs? What fears do I have surrounding allowing someone to have different beliefs than I do?

Thinking about the term "constructive criticism" make me feel:

_____

_____

_____

_____

_____

_____

_____

_____

_____

_____

_____

_____

_____

_____

The most difficult emotion for me to deal with is _____, it causes me to...

The last time I witnessed destructive behavior in someone else was _____ and
I felt _____.

The last time I experienced destructive behavior <u>myself</u> was _____, and I felt _____.

I usually complain about _____ but I actually like it because it makes me feel
_____.

This is what is frustrating to me today, this is a positive affirmation I can make from this situation:

Being successful in this life isn't all puppies and kittens. It actually can be annoying because:

Internally, I like to allow certain people to push my buttons because:

This is a time that I tried to manipulate a situation and how I feel about it now:

There are so many times I have felt used. However, the good thing about being used is:

_____

_____

_____

_____

_____

_____

_____

_____

_____

_____

_____

_____

_____

_____

_____

_____

How often do I feel judged? This is how I tell if it's real or imagined:

_____

_____

_____

_____

_____

_____

_____

_____

_____

_____

_____

_____

_____

_____

_____

_____

When people are perky and bubbly I don't like it because _____. What I think this says about me:

_____

_____

_____

_____

_____

_____

_____

_____

_____

_____

_____

_____

_____

_____

_____

This is a time I escaped my responsibilities_____, I did it because _____ and these were the results:

What do I fear the most? Why? Is my fear rational?

A difficult memory and the coping mechanisms I used at the time. I could have done this instead:

This is the last time I cried and why:

Write a letter to the future YOU.

Write a letter to you at age 10

Write down a list of "regrets", next, write a check mark at each one that you had control over and a heart by the ones that were out of your hands.

This was the worst day of my life and what it has taught me.

An incredibly difficult choice I've had to make in my life is:

What love means to me (in detail). Where did I learn these attributes?

Something I've done that required someone to forgive me, write a letter of forgiveness to myself for that.

What smell is disgusting to me? Why?

What type of music can I not stand to listen to? What about it turns me off? Do I see these things in myself, where?

What risks do you want to take? What's holding you back?

What items/objects do I find the most comforting? Why do I think that is?

Something that really frustrates me and how I usually react to it is…

A place I'd like to travel that I don't think I will go is_____ What's stopping me?

Something I do to make myself feel better that might be a little toxic is:

The worst home I've ever lived in was_____ How I'm going to stop
that from happening again is…

_____

_____

_____

_____

_____

_____

_____

_____

_____

_____

_____

_____

_____

_____

_____

_____

What I am most motivated by and how I feel about that:

The one thing I worry about most often is _____ what is true and untrue about my fear?

_____

_____

_____

_____

_____

_____

_____

_____

_____

_____

_____

_____

_____

_____

_____

_____

My favorite outfit is _____ when I wear it, I feel…

A secret I have hidden is _____. How has it affected my life?

What I perceive as the worst thing I've ever done is…

The last argument I was in was about _____, looking back on it I feel:

The longest grudge I've ever held was about _____. Should I have let it go sooner? What did I gain or lose from this situation?

I usually lie to myself about _____. With that acknowledged, how can I stop avoiding the truth?

When I was a child I wanted to be _____ when I grew up. How can I bring that into my current life?

When someone elicits a reaction from me, I can see myself in them because:

Something I was in denial about and what brought me into accepting it is:

An unfavorable label people sometimes give me is (bossy, lazy, boring etc,) how does this label shape my personality?

I tend to judge people when they _____. Do I sometimes do that thing? Why is it OK for me but not others?

My current role in life is (wife, student, mom, caretaker, etc) however, I am also:

A question I would ask my future self is?

My favorite safe space is_____ because:

_____

_____

_____

_____

_____

_____

_____

_____

_____

_____

_____

_____

_____

_____

_____

_____

Something I want people to know about me that I have trouble telling them is…

When I hold my hand over my heart and say "Thank you" the first things that come to mind are…

My least favorite part of the day is _____ because:

_____

_____

_____

_____

_____

_____

_____

_____

_____

_____

_____

_____

_____

_____

_____

My favorite part of the day is _____ because...

_____

_____

_____

_____

_____

_____

_____

_____

_____

_____

_____

_____

_____

_____

Was my favorite part of the day journal entry longer than my <u>least</u> favorite? How can I balance them?

The best compliment I've ever received is_____. I don't believe it though and here's why…

If I could name my biggest weakness, it would be this. It started when….

I just need to get this off my chest! (Rant away!)

What I miss most about my childhood and why.

What I want to hear from my loved ones that I'm afraid to ask for. Will I ever ask for it?

Something I struggled to accept about myself and how I began to accept it is…

When I have time alone I usually feel _____

My biggest "What if" moment is _____ and what if I did it now?

_____

_____

_____

_____

_____

_____

_____

_____

_____

_____

_____

_____

_____

_____

_____

_____

Is there someone I miss a great deal? How does missing them affect my life?

My most memorable birthday is _____, what stands out most now is:

How can I use my fears to fuel my desire to achieve a goal?

I judge myself about _____. Has someone else ever judged me by this?

I'm really embarrassed to admit that I am really good at:

What about my culture am I least proud of and why?

My least favorite responsibility and how I manage to do it anyway is…

_____

_____

_____

_____

_____

_____

_____

_____

_____

_____

_____

_____

_____

_____

_____

_____

_____

_____

As a child, if I was scared/hurt, my parents (or other caretakers) responded…

Here's a secret from my childhood that I've never told anyone.

What messages was I given in childhood about who I was "supposed" to be? Did I try to do that? What was the outcome?

How do I comfort myself? How often do I succeed, what does it mean if I can't?

As a child, how did people respond when I tried to show my talents? How does this affect me now?

I give myself permission to….

_____

_____

_____

_____

_____

_____

_____

_____

_____

_____

_____

_____

_____

_____

_____

_____

_____

In what ways do I hold myself to a higher standard than others?

How do I react when something doesn't go the way I want?

You have reached the of this journal but not the end of this journey! Shadow work is never done, you will always reach more of yourself!
If you enjoyed this journal and would like to see a second installment. Please let me know in your Amazon review and make sure to check the author page for other helpful books.

Peace to you on your healing journey!

Made in the USA
Las Vegas, NV
11 February 2021